P9-CEU-381

JAPAN

Marion Sichel

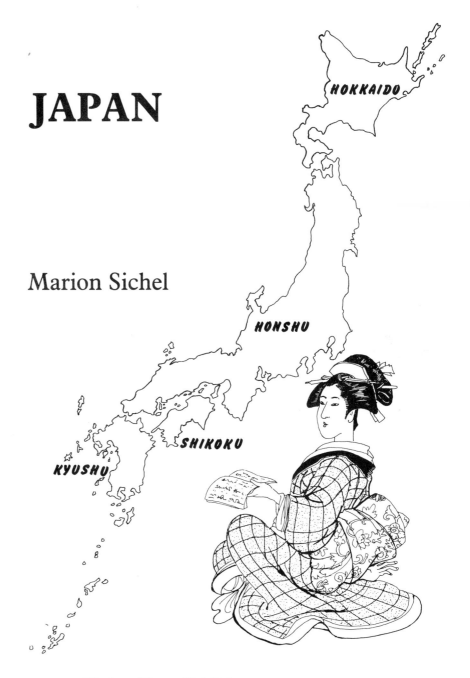

HOKKAIDO

HONSHU

SHIKOKU

KYUSHU

Chelsea House Publishers
New York · New Haven · Philadelphia

© Marion Sichel 1987
First published 1987

Printed in Great Britain
Published in the U.S.A. by
Chelsea House Publishers
5014 West Chester Pike
Edgemont, Pa., 19028

Published in the U.K. by
B.T. Batsford Limited
4 Fitzhardinge Street,
London W1H 0AH

Library of Congress Cataloging-in-Publication Data

Sichel, Marion.
    Japan.

    (National costume reference)
    Bibliography: p.
    Includes index.
    Summary: Describes the traditional dress of Japan
and explores the historical, religious, and social
contexts in which it is appropriately worn.
    1. Costume—Japan—Juvenile literature. [1. Costume—
Japan.   2. Japan—Social life and customs]   I. Title.
II. Series.
GT1560.S53   1988   391'.00952   87–15120
ISBN 1–55546–742–3

*Nobleman in informal attire, with
long full sleeves*

Jacket illustration

Background: *Satin kimono of early
seventeenth century with design of wood sorrel
leaves*
Left: *Man wearing kimono and haori in
matching colour, and traditional geta footwear*
Centre: *Ainu chieftain from Hokkaidō
wearing kimono woven from elm bark fibre.
Round his head is a plaited grass fibre band
and on his lap is a prayer wheel*
Right: *Woman wearing a hand-painted ro
gauze hōmongi with an unlined obi*

CONTENTS

Preface   4
Introduction   5

Early and everyday dress   11
The kimono   17
The obi   22
Court and ceremonial dress   24
The samurai   28
The Ainu   35
Geisha girls   38
Nō and Kabuki theatre costume   40
Children   50
Tattooing   53
Headwear and hairstyles   54
Footwear   57

Glossary of costume terms   59
Bibliography   63
Index   64

Above
*Wandering street musician playing
the traditional* gekkin

*A devotee of Buddha wearing a
drum bow*

PREFACE

Japan, although now culturally influenced by both East and West, still has its own unique national costume. Due to climatic conditions dress has always been influenced by the requirement of airiness to counter the humidity. Therefore wide-sleeved and wrap-over garments are in everyday usage.

The loose style of the *kimono* has been found to be the most comfortable, giving complete freedom of movement.

Although Western dress has been generally adopted in public life, the *kimono* still tends to be worn on special occasions and by many women; also by many older men who, when returning from work, change into more comfortable attire. Western dress, although more practical for work, is unsuitable for the Japanese way of kneeling and sitting on the floor.

The traditional patterns incorporating flowers, especially cherry, plum and almond blossom, represent the characteristics of the country, as do designs based on the four seasons, and many of these are combined in their fabrics.

The numerous illustrations in this volume depict many of these designs and their variations.

Special thanks are due to Mrs A. Shindo at the Japanese Embassy for her help in reading the typescript.

Man in kimono *and* haori, *the sleeves also serve as pockets. He is wearing* geta

Tea was introduced from China in the ninth century. This shows a young Buddhist grinding the fragrant tea leaves

A Kabuki towel dance based on a Nō play telling the story of a princess who has been shunned in love

INTRODUCTION

Headwear of a Buddhist priest

Japan is part of a long chain of some 4,000 small islands in the north Pacific Ocean stretching about 4,828 kilometres from the most northerly Kurile Islands to Taiwan in the south, lying off the east coast of Asia from which it is separated by the Sea of Japan.

The four largest islands are Hokkaidō (also known as Yezo) in the north, Honshū the main island, Shikoku and Kyūshū.

The islands are the most mountainous in the world and have over fifty active volcanoes, many sulphur springs, and are subject to earthquakes. The graceful curve of the snow-capped, but no longer active volcano, Mount Fuji on the island of Honshū, is one of the most beautiful mountains in the world, with a prominent place in Japanese decorative art. The valleys are covered in woodlands, and the vegetation is lush and beautiful. Short and fast flowing rivers descend steeply from the mountains, too swift for navigation, but the coastlines have some good harbours. The chief ports are Yokohama, Nagasaki and Osaka.

The climate from the most northerly islands to the most southerly varies considerably. There is much rainfall causing humidity but nowhere is the heat intense although the northern winters can be very cold.

Agriculture is an important industry, growing rice, cereals, tea, coffee and fruit but the manufacture of porcelain, laquer-work and silks is extensive and such goods are widely exported.

The primitive religious belief was that the gods and their offspring peopled the earth, thus giving rise to Shintō (the way of the gods) which is a mixture of ancestor and nature worship. In the sixth century Buddhism reached Japan from China and the two creeds remained distinct until the ninth century when Shintō worship was absorbed into Buddhism, but its own beliefs survived as well as its great festivals.

The greatest festival of the year is *Obon*, held in the middle of August, commemorates the temporary return to earth of the ancestral spirits.

Young girl gathering in the rice harvest

Japanese mummers dressed in
traditional attire, singing and
dancing a comic folk dance known as
the Manzai

These festival costumes feature the
pagentry of the Hollyhock Festival
during the Imperial Heian period
(794-1192)

Young lady kneeling to play the
samisen, a traditional instrument
originally from Manila

Young girl in a brightly coloured kimono *and straw hat, singing at the Rice Planting Festival*

A shrine maiden welcoming visitors to a Shintō shrine

Setsubun celebrates the end of winter and the beginning of spring when, wearing brightly coloured *kimono*, the people drive out evil spirits and encourage the good ones.

The New Year Festival, *Oshogatsu*, is a national holiday, when dressed in fine *kimono* the people visit the shrines and temples and have great feastings.

Although maybe a mythical figure and the date an arbitrary one, the first emperor, crowned in 660 BC, was supposed to have been the great-grandson of the Sun Goddess, and was given the posthumous title of Jimmu, meaning 'divine warrior'. His descendants have ruled and continue to rule with unbroken succession, although from the twelfth to the nineteenth centuries military dictators with the title *Sei-i-tai shogun*, meaning barbarian-repressing general, were the dominant powers until their overthrow in 1868 when the Meiji was fully restored and feudalism abolished.

National costumes owe their characteristics to such factors as environment, climate, class, development and convention.

Japan was isolated from the rest of the world for over two hundred years during the shogunate, but during this time there was a great deal of internal economic expansion, the Japanese being a highly literate and progressive people. Their dress and other traditions have therefore survived and many of these are to be seen in folk art and in their plays as part of their national heritage.

Although they sought Chinese culture from the earliest days of their national existence, and Western culture and technology after the restoration of the Mikado in 1868, the Japanese have enjoyed a continuity of tradition with few changes.

The Japanese belong to the Mongolian race, which includes Koreans, Manchurians, Chinese and Ainu. They are generally petite, good looking with a comparatively flat plane of face, and graceful, with yellow to light olive complexions. The general physical characteristics are straight black hair, with oblique eyelids which are distinctive to their race, and dark to black-brown eyes.

It is generally agreed that Ainu were the original inhabitants of the archepelago who although now a dwindling race are mainly confined to the northern islands. They are distinguishable from other inhabitants by their profusion of black hair and the long beards of the men.

Rice Planting Festival for which the participants are dressed in brightly coloured kimono and peaked round straw hats

A Shintō priest

A Shintō priest carrying a simple shrine on his back, selling charms

The gohei, an ancient Shintō symbol made of paper in a zigzag pattern fastened to a sacred stick, being offered to spirits of the departed

Buddhist priest heading a funeral procession

A pilgrim paying homage at a Buddhist shrine

Abbess of a nunnery in Nara, with her head shaven

Young Buddhist priest at the shrine of the Tokugawa shogunate at Nikko

A Buddhist priest seated in meditation and prayer

Young girl kneeling, playing the traditional gekkin

The hereditory and dedicated warriors – the samurai – are so much part of the Japanese history that they and their uniforms must be included in this book, likewise the fascinating dress associated with the traditional Nō and Kabuki theatres. The Nō plays reflect the Buddhist view of the world and convey, through mime, stylised dance and chanting, universal themes. The Kabuki provide a more spectacular form of drama with dialogue.

From a study of the geography, history, social customs and religious beliefs of the Japanese, can be seen and appreciated their unique traditional costume, the *kimono* and its variations, as well as their characteristic hairstyles and footwear.

The Japanese language is one of the most difficult in the world, the written word consisting of ideograms for which there are at least two pronunciations for each character.

In the early times there was no distinction in dress between the sexes, age or class. But in the seventeeth century a tight class system divided the people into four distinct categories and they had to wear clothes in the styles and colours prescribed to them; failure to comply being a punishable offence.

In spite of this repression, freedom of dress remained in the theatre, and the prostitutes were still permitted their strikingly designed attire. These latter were confined to licensed pleasure areas which became the centres of fashion, and the ordinary women secretly copied the designs that originated from them, for instance multi-coloured stripes and chessboard patterns as well as tie-dye designs.

Classification began at the top with the warrior class or samurai who enjoyed many privileges, but also had responsibilities and were expected to set a good example. The farmers, who formed the majority of the population, were in the second position due to the importance of their contribution to the necessities of life; they were followed by the craftsmen and lastly the merchants. But during the late 1860s wealth, which had previously been measured by the quantity of rice a samurai would need in one year, became based on a currency of copper, silver and gold. This led to the rise of the merchants in the heirarchy and the decline of the class system.

A flute player, his head concealed by his bamboo headwear

10

EARLY AND EVERYDAY DRESS

From pre-historic times Japanese dress was made of two pieces of cloth sewn together front and back, and held in place with a cord or sash around the waist. At first it consisted of two separate parts: upper and lower garments.

Originally the upper garment, worn by men and women, was a simple linen or caftan type shirt with close-cut sleeves and an opening in the front. Loose trousers formed the lower garment for men. Women had long pleated skirts known as *mo*. A smock and a pair of cotton trousers tight above the calf, just like knickerbockers, could also be worn. Over the smock they sometimes wore a very full jacket with wide sleeves split at the shoulders and down the sides, and with a close fitting collar.

Whilst working, men wore a *nae-eboshi*, a soft black hat, not unlike a night-cap in shape. They often went bare footed, but for walking a long distance *ashinaka* or straw sandals were worn. These protected only the soles of the feet and were worn with cloth or straw leggings, sometimes held in place by a piece of string looped around the big toe. In rainy weather, *geta* or wooden clogs were worn. These were made higher by means of transverse strips of wood and held on to the feet by two straps passing between the toes and over the top of the foot.

Labourers wore dark coloured trousers with a knee-length coat known as a *happi*, and wooden clogs *or geta*. They also wore an everyday *kimono* made of smoke blue and white striped cotton.

The *happi* usually had the family crest or guild mark embroidered on the back. Those worn by sedan-chair bearers were mostly indigo, edged with red, and made of a coarse unlined cotton.

Servants had a form of uniform, generally consisting of a pair of breeches and horizonatal stripes, and bright flowered jackets, whose patterns and colours were more dependent on the material available than on a prevailing fashion. In summer, when engaged in domestic or agricultural work they shed their

Man dressed in a happi *attending the*
Gion Festival in Kyoto

11

A fisherman

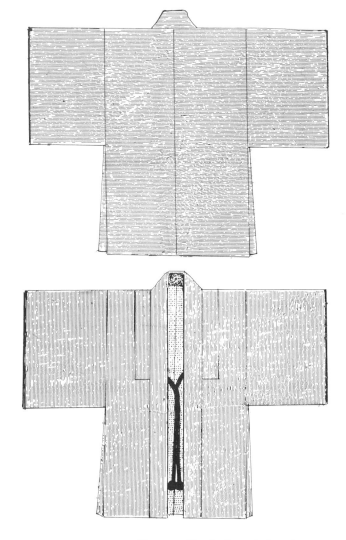

Front and back view of a haori worn
over a kimono. The material is
slightly padded with an interwoven
pattern, the lining of silk crepe.
Typically it has a seam at the back
and the fastening is made of plaited
silk cords

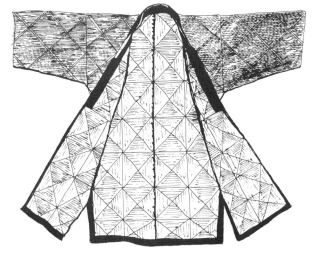

A fisherman's sashiko jacket in light
and dark blue material sewn together
in a trellis pattern, specially designed
to resist the elements

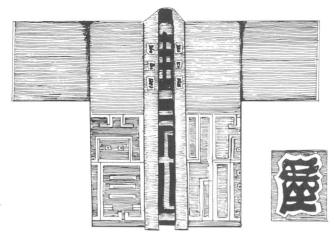

Loose happi *as worn by a sedan-chair bearer, it is made of coarse cotton and is unlined. The detail is of the writing which is identical on either side of the neck edging*

A carrying pad or bandori, *the word means 'sparrow'; so called because they give the bearer a bird-like appearance. These pads are used to cushion the weight of heavy loads carried on the back*

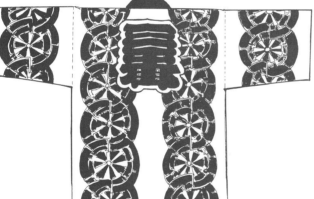

The short cotton happi *can be worn on festive occasions nowadays. It was originally regarded as working clothes worn by lower ranking samurai. It developed from a silk* haori, *a jacket worn by men over the* kimono *and* hakama

Back view of a happi. *They are usually dyed dark blue, and on the back is printed the crest or trade mark of the wearer's employer, the design varying according to the status of the wearer*

13

jackets and worked stripped to the waist or removed all their garments apart from a loin cloth. The women too, who worked in the fields, stripped to the waist; exposure of the breasts being readily accepted in the early days.

As trousers were more practical for farming, these were worn with cotton *kimono*, and were supported by a sash and braces. Straw sandals held on with ribbon straps, or wooden clogs, were worn. In winter they used snow boots made of plaited straw. Hunters, like warriors, wore leather shoes or boots.

Working women wore a simple *kimono* wrapped over and drawn in at the waist by a *yumaki* or narrow girdle to which was attached a kind of shirt-cum-apron which served to protect the *kimono*. The number of *kimono* worn one over the other depended upon the weather and also on the influence of the wearer.

The boat women who worked on the many rivers and between the islands wore patterned *kimono* and flat straw hats fastening under the chin. Girls from the Kyoto region had simple decorated kerchiefs with a cushion made out of water-side plants to enable them to carry such things as farm produce on their heads.

A woman from Kagoshima, south Kyūshū, carrying a giant horseradish on her head. These could weigh up to 45 kg

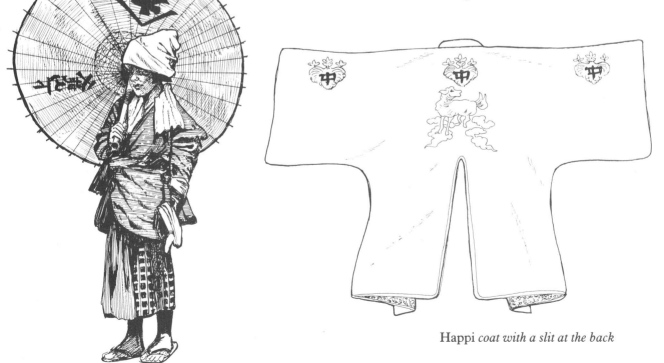

Japanese peasant girl carrying a large paper and bamboo umbrella

Happi *coat with a slit at the back*

Early type of hakama *worn mainly by men*

Huntsman of the Hida mountains

A *katsugi* was generally a cloth worn on the head. The name came to be used for an outer garment worn by women of nobility when outdoors and was designed to cover their heads and faces, but it could also be just an over-robe without the head covering.

People protected themselves from rain by using either a folding or flat umbrella made of bamboo, paper or oiled cloth.

In winter a *mino* or loose cloak made of lengths of straw sewn together was worn. In snowy regions the *mino* were fitted with hoods.

In medieval times the *koshimaki* or waist wrap was a skirt worn by women servants, but by the seventeeth century it had evolved into a full-length garment worn by samurai ladies for ceremonial attire.

Fabrics were generally dyed a shade of indigo produced from the fermentation of leaves of the ai bean, violet from crushed root of bugloss or murasaki, or dark red from the root of madder-wort.

From as early as the eighth century various methods of fabric dyeing had been used, but the simple tie-dyeing and stencils were discarded as brocade weaving was developed. But another dyeing method prevailed, *tsujigahana*, which was more effective than the block printing or simple tie-dyeing of previous times. This was a technique of dyeing and hand painting with ink and coloured pigments.

Historically Japanese dress derived from the *kosodo* or small sleeved garment. This was originally a plain undergarment worn by the majority of the people, but gradually it was much more decorated and became a garment worn by nobles and officials. The *kosode* gradually evolved into a *kimono* on which the *obi* or sash was the prominent feature.

Due to the lack of interest in emphasising the shape of the figure, more emphasis was laid on decoration, and the great variety of techniques and skills of application of these elaborate designs has led to the *kimono* being one of the most artistic forms of Japanese crafts. The *kasane-gi* or layered robes with their long trains concealed the body, whilst the narrow *kosode* allowed the physical shape of the woman to be seen.

Kimono can be of any colour with striped patterns, dots or checks, geometrical designs, or with animal, bird or floral motifs. Men's *kimono* are more sombre in colour, the more popular ones being black, brown, grey or dark blue. But Japanese dress is always graceful and picturesque. It remains unaffected by the fashions of the day and is never subjected to gaudy colours, nor to glittering ornamentation.

Kata-suso, meaning shoulders and hem, is a style where the design is placed only at the hem and shoulders, leaving the remainder plain. This type of *kosode* worn with an *obi* called for little decoration.

Winter robes are very thick, lined with swansdown, and the *kosode* is worn in greater number. When at home a *kosode* and a full length *kimono* of transparent gauze may well be worn over a *hakama* or overtrousers. Hunting outfits called *kariginu*, had narrow sleeves which were attached only beneath the arms. They had strings at the cuffs to close them for easier manoeuvrability when on horseback and when using the bow and arrow.

Hunting outfit, known as kariginu, *the sleeves of which could be closed at the cuffs with strings*

White kosode *with nuihaku design*

The suikan, *similar to the* kariginu, *but less formal with a stand-up collar tied on the right. It could be worn as a formal gown by the lower classes. Towards the end of the twelfth century it also acted as ceremonial dress for warriors*

16

Early style of kimono *shortened by pulling up and tying it in place*

THE KIMONO

The word *kimono* (both singular and plural) means 'a thing worn': *mono* = a thing and kiru = worn.

Artistically and technically the *kimono* is one of the most aesthetic of the national costumes in the world, its beauty being fully appreciated only when worn. Although not of Japanese origin, its great appeal is attributed to seventeeth and eighteenth century Japanese designers.

In contrast to western style dress the *kimono*, from the most formal to the most casual, is of the same form. The *obi* or sash is an expression of beauty, and both the *kimono* and *obi* emphasise the beauty of straight lines.

The *kimono* is a long gown with expansive sleeves set at right angles, and they can also serve as pockets. It has a V-neck without buttons or ties, being lapped left over right and crossed over the chest and secured at the waist with a sash or *obi*.

For everyday, men and women wear the *kimono*, a garment with many variations dating back to the eighth century. It is worn mainly in the home, the very informal *kimono* having shorter sleeves than the conventional styles. Women's and men's are similar except that the hemline and sleeves of the women's are slightly longer, and the hem may be quilted. It consists of four parts: sleeves, body, gusset and a neckband that is replaceable. It is unlined for the summer, but for the cold winter it is warmly padded.

All *kimono* are of a standard shape, with small variations, enabling men and women of all heights to wear them, a versatility not found in western dress. Types of *kimono* take their names from the way in which textiles are dyed or woven, several methods sometimes being combined.

The *kosode* or small sleeve is distinct from the larger sleeve *osode*, wide sleeve *hirosode*, and the long hanging sleeve *furisode*, all of which remain fashionable today.

In the *hirosode* type of garment, the end of the sleeve is left completely open whereas in the *kosode* the lower part is sewn

A kosode *of the seventeeth century, the style combining the tubular style of sleeve of a* kimono *worn by farmers and the* kosode *of the upper class worn with a simple braided cord* obi

up, leaving just a small opening for the arm to protrude. The *kosode* sleeves are generally narrower and shorter than those of the *hirosode*. The wide sleeves of the *hirosode* were very popular particularly by the noblemen from the early ninth to the late twelfth centuries. The skirts of these *kimono* were long and impractical, so they were worn mainly by the wealthy, although copied by the general populace. Despite numerous edicts passed limiting the width of sleeves, these edicts were continuously ignored.

The length of the kimono sleeve is measured from shoulder to cuff with the arm outstretched horizontally. The width is measured vertically from the top to bottom of the sleeve, and this may be greater than the length. The very wide sleeves of the *furisode* have about one quarter of their width left open.

When wide sleeves were fashionable, the poorer classes could only afford the narrower ones, so while the term *kosode* was used for an undergarment by the nobility, the narrower sleeves were still associated with the poorer, but later when the *kosode* developed into formal wear, it took on a certain charm.

As the people wished to vary their dress, but had limited resources, they resolved this by taking two *kimono* of different designs, dividing them and joining the left half of one to the right half of another and vice versa, thus making two new ones. This also had the advantage of discarding the worn parts. This idea went back to the eighth century and was a means of creating many new designs. Once divided vertically, horizontal divisions were also combined, giving a chequered pattern. This was known as *dangawari* meaning stepwise.

For semi-formal wear this tie-dyed kimono *is worn for visiting, with a back* fukuro obi *in a tapestry weave of a peony design*

Yellow plaid kimono: *The cloth is woven by hand and the dye made of a special grass*

18

A man's kimono dress coat of ▶
patterned half silk with a soft lining
and a seam down the centre back. the
lapels are slightly padded and this
style is worn with a belt. The sleeves
set at right angles also act as pockets.
A woman's has slightly longer sleeves
and a quilted hem at the base

◀ A tsukesage kimono with hand-
painted design, worn for tea
gatherings, concerts and similar
semi-formal occasions

◀ A yukata, summer kimono, of
unlined cotton traditionally put on
after a hot bath. It is usually of navy
blue and white designs and gives the
impression of coolness

A satin furisode with full length ▶
sleeves with hand-painted designs
and fine embroidery. The obi has a
diamond design of pine needles
picked out in gold thread. The
obiage is in a tie-dye design. The
costume is suitable for any formal
social occasion as well as for
weddings

19

Appliqué designs with different fabrics was another popular way of varying the designs economically.

New techniques during the seventeeth century enabled both sides of the cloth to show the pattern, even on fine materials. Several techniques could be used in combination with each other. These led to experimentation with overlapping designs.

Motifs of every description and size, stylised or realistic were used often confined to the borders and shoulders of a garment, or could form an overall pattern. From the late seventeeth century when the broad *obi* was fashionable, the designs on the gowns became more distinct between the upper and lower parts.

These designs could be repeating or related motifs or a single subject such as a scene, but these are less popular than the large motifs starting from a corner and creating an asymmetric pattern.

During the sixteenth and seventeenth centuries figured and flowered fabrics were in wide demand.

In the mid-sixteenth century weaving shops flourished in Japan and produced a great variety of silks and brocades with raised ornamentation in the Chinese style, as well as *nuihaku* which was embroidery with gold and silver foil appliqué, or embroidery with stencilling which gave the rich and dense effects required.

Foreign influences in the textile designs came from the small Kyushu islands and also from the painted chintzes introduced by Portuguese traders. These promoted animal and vegetable designs and large scale patterns and realistic details of garden or landscape which became popular as well.

Ornamentation could be introduced obliquely, leaving large areas blank. In *kata-suso* or shoulder and skirt design, only the upper and lower quarters of the kosode were ornamented, the two parts corresponding to give a complete view.

The making up of the garments did not interfere in any way with an entire design. The more formal the garment, the stiffer and more angular it became and an unwillingness to cut into elaborate weaves no doubt influenced the designs.

The year is divided into three seasons for the changes in apparel. Colour combinations are extremely important and certain colours are traditionally linked to the months or seasons, for example from November to February it is traditional to wear a white *kimono* with plum red lining, in March and April lavender with a blue lining, whilst yellow and

The semi-formal tsukesage kimono *with a colourful chrysanthemum design. Over the* obi *can be seen the* obi cord *or* obi-jime

20

orange are the colours for winter and spring. These colours mirror the seasons as do the designs, such as cherry blossom for spring, snow scenes or plum blossom for winter; and summer and autumn depicted by ocean waves and red maple leaves.

A *kimono* for summer wear, known as a *yukata* and worn over an undergarment, is of a light cotton, whilst for spring and autumn it is lined, but in the winter it is also padded for warmth. The wadded *kimono* is called a *water-ire*. A short coat or *haori*, also lined, may be worn over a *kimono* for extra warmth outdoors, or for formal occasions, the sleeves of which can also act as pockets.

Kimono worn by children are made with tucks at the shoulders and waist, so that as they grow the *kimono* can be lengthened.

Kimono are most commonly made of linen, cotton or silk, cotton being the more popular for everyday wear, silk being worn only on special occasions. The latter are cared for meticulously, each piece being unpicked and cleaned separately and then re-sewn.

For weddings a very elaborate and colourful *furisode kimono* is worn over one of white or of pastel shades. A tasselled fan may be tucked into the *obi* and the butterfly bow padded with a small cushion or *obi-age*.

The hairstyle is especially complicated with a white or pastel coloured hat decorated at the back and topped with flowers and ribbons. The bridegroom wears a jacket with his crest over the *kimono* as well as a special pleated skirt, the *hakama*.

For funerals, in many regions, a *kimono* bearing the family crest, with a wide *obi*, is worn, although the colour for mourning amongst the Shintō is white.

The kimono *tucked in at the waist, with raised hems and shorter sleeves, worn with high shoes. A style from the mid eighteenth century to the early twentieth*

Little girl kneeling wearing a kimono

21

THE OBI

The *kimono* is kept in place with an *obi* which is a wide sash that is wound twice around the waist. For men this is usually in the form of a narrow band of white or black crepe for informal wear and of corded silk, or brocade for more formal occasions. The *obi* is the most costly part of a woman's wardrobe. The fabrics, colours and designs are dependent on the seasons as well as whether the women are married or single. It is often made of gold brocade for formal occasions and of satin, figured crepe and corded silk for everyday wear. Their width can vary as well as the many ways of tying them; for example a double drum bow worn by married women on ceremonial occasions, which signifies the doubling of joy. Another, for unmarried women, the plump sparrow which looks like a bird with spread wings.

The fukuro (*double-folded*) obi *made of brocade, using gold and silver threads depicting a flower. Bird or geometrical designs are also popular*

Until about the end of the fifteenth century the *obi* was just a thin cord; its function to tie the gown in place. It then became a broader braid or plaited cord which was wound around the waist three to four times with a long tassel decoration.

From mid seventeenth century, when the *kimono* became longer, the *obi* for women became wider. Until this time it was tied either front, back or side, but then it became fashionable for single girls to tie the *obi* at the back, whilst married women tied theirs in the front. A young girl's *obi* is tied with the ends sometimes standing as high as her shoulders.

With the fashion for realistic pictorial ornamentation on the *kimono* the *obi* too was decorated on one or both sides, or only on visible areas.

The Kabuki actors had a great influence on the styles of bows, for instance the *tateya* or standing arrow, and the *chidori* or plover bow.

The *obi* took its present form during the mid eighteenth century, when it measured about four metres in length and was about one metre wide, although nowadays it is often narrower. It is folded lengthwise, doubled and sewn along one edge, the ends tied in a flat bow at the back.

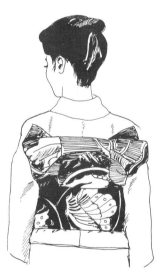

Straight line box bow for ceremonial and formal wear

The *obi* is made to project at the back with a pad tied on by a crepe scarf in front and a white silk cord or brocade band tying the ends down at the back, under the bow, and fastening in front with a gold or jewelled clasp or brooch decoration. This *obi-jime* emphasises the beauty of both the *obi* and the *kimono*.

A plain kimono *is worn with a black* obi *for mourning*

Arrow bow for everyday wear

Fashionable actor or courtisan ▼ *wearing a* furisode kimono *with a large* obi

Young girl wearing a colourful drum ▶ obi *in a double fold*

◀ *From the mid nineteenth century the* obis *were short and the bows simpler*

23

COURT AND
CEREMONIAL DRESS

The court robe, a typical Chinese style of dress, is possibly the origin of the *kimono*. It consists of a full upper garment, slit either side, with a stand-up collar, worn over long loose trousers held up with a sash, the ends hanging down in front.

For men the court dress consisted of long trailing trousers beneath a *kimono* dress coat, known as a *water-ire* of which a vertical seam at centre back is a typical feature. It is also lightly padded with cotton wool and floss silk between the soft silk crepe lining and the external material. Fastenings may be made of plaited silk cords and the full sleeves act as pockets. Several of these coats may be worn, one over the other, as Japanese houses with their paper screen walls tend to be cold.

A *kimono* is classified by the occasion and by whom it is worn. One of the most formal and striking of kimono designs is the five family crests in white on a black background, worn with a white under-kimono. A double folded ornamental *obi*, bustle sash (*obi-age*) and cord (*obi-jime*) and gold and silver *zori* complete the outfit.

Court ladies wore the *iro tomosode*, which is a more colourful version of the *kurotomosode*. Until the seventeenth century the *uchikake*, a full length outer robe worn by noblewomen on ceremonial occasions, became the traditional bridal dress.

A man's ceremonial dress consists of a *kimono*, usually made of dark blue silk, and a pleated and divided skirt, the *hakama*, made in fine stripes. Over this a loose coat with the family crest embroidered in white is also worn. A belt around the hips and a silk cord with tasselled ends around the neck completes the attire for courtiers as well as the samurai.

A Chinese style of costume, the upper garment slit at the sides. The trousers are held in place with a sash fastening in front

A silk uchikake *embroidered with poems. These are so placed to avoid repeating any juxtaposition*

The uchikake, *the sixteenth century ceremonial winter robe is now a most formal bride attire*

The coloured tomosode kimono *is less formal than the black, but also has five crests, and often has designs at the shoulders and sleeves as well as at the skirt*

Nobleman wearing a long trailing robe or osode *which has large open sleeves*

Man in haori *and* hakama *wearing* tabi *and* zori

An uchikake *worn over a* kosode *with a small purse inserted between the front panels of the collar*

Formal black tomosode kimono *with five crests. The white undergarment accentuates the lines of the kimono, the collar of which could be embroidered with silver thread. The* fukuro obi *is of a damask weave and the* obiage *of a tie-dye design. The* obi-jime *is of a silk covered or braid cord. Zori are worn with this outfit*

In winter or cooler weather, it was necessary to wear several *kimono*, one over the other. This phenomenon, a distinctive feature of Japanese culture, was seen most forceably from the early ninth to the late twelfth centuries when court ladies wore up to twelve layers of *kimono* for ceremonial occasions. It was important for the colours to be in harmony as each layer was visible at the neck, sleeves and at the bottom of the skirt. this multi-layered robe is known as *juni-hitoe*. The seasons and occasion played an important part in the colour schemes.

Noblemen vied with each other for elegance. They wore long trailing robes with large open sleeves and beneath these a *kosode*. Ranks at court were mainly distinguished by wearing a hat of silken material, lacquered and stiffened. This was called a *kammuri*. A kind of skull cap was also worn, at the back of which rose a tube, about 15 cm high, enclosing a bunch of hair at the crown of the head. This stiffened tube was tied tightly at its base and held the tuft of hair securely in place. Finally two flat pigtails, woven with horse-hair or with lacquered silk gauze hung down the back.

A dobuko, *short coat, similar to a* haori. *Originally the dress of street vendors, but towards the end of the sixteenth century worn informally by the upper class men*

Noblewoman's multi-layered robe or juni-hitoe, *with an* hakama *worn beneath*

THE SAMURAI

The illustrious Heian period came to an end in 1184 with the rise of the powerful military families, and in 1185 when the Taira was defeated by the Mimamoto family, Kamakura in eastern Japan became the seat of the shogunate, although Kyoto remained the seat of the Imperial Court.

The Kyoto style of *kimono* was regarded as too lavish and impractical for the samurai class and the simpler *kamakura* style evolved.

An adaption of farmers' dress which allowed for free movement, the *hitatare*, became everyday wear for warriors, likewise the *hakama* worn with a short upper garment with the cuffs closing with strings when required.

Ceremonial dress, the *yoroi-hitatare*, with narrower sleeves and short trousers and leggings could be worn with armour (*yoroi*).

Hitatare, *everyday wear for warriors, adapted from farmers' dress to allow for free movement*

The dress of the samurai women was in principle fairly simple, although once the samurai class had cbtained power it became more elaborate, and the *kosode* gradually became more colourful.

From the twelfth to the fourteenth centuries, the women instead of wearing the multi-layered robe, the *juni-hitoe*, wore a *kosode* over the *hakama*, which had until then been regarded as an undergarment. the sleeves of the *kosode*, which had previously been open at the end, were made smaller by being partially sewn up, this being the origin of the more modern kimono.

The samurai women disliked to show their faces in public so wore veils or elaborate headdresses resembling umbrellas.

To shorten their kimonos, they held them up with a sash around their chest, on which prayers were written.

With the rise of the warriors and the wealthy *daimyō* (feudal chiefs) to higher positions, a more elaborate *kimono* and a small purse tucked between the front *kimono* panels, just above the breast, was favoured by the wives on ceremonial occasions, although the *kosode* was still worn.

A samurai in full armour carrying two swords

The wooden scabbard is decorated with lacquer and partially wrapped in silk bands. This style of mounting for a sling sword first appeared in the fifteenth century

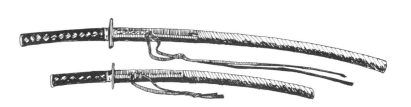

Two swords with dragon designs. The wooden scabbards have a ribbed carving decoration and the wood hilts are wrapped with silk bands

Sword guard with floral and cloud design

Sword guard with a design of pine trees

Retainer's robe, a daimon, *similar to the* suō. *It has five family crests: one on each shoulder, one on each sleeve and one at the back of the neck. The* eboshi *cap is also worn*

Ceremonial dress for generals, the yoroi-hitatare *was worn with short trousers and leggings. The sleeves were not so wide, and armour, or* yoroi *could be worn over this dress*

29

A samurai wearing a kami-shimo, *a derivative of a* kataginu *with a* naga-hakama *trailing the ground, for a ceremonial occasion*

Iron scale armour

A samurai in marching order with the trousers pulled up

◄ *A samurai dressed in ceremonial attire for the Gion festival, wearing a* kataginu *and* hakama

A samurai dressed in a combination of kimono, kami-shimo, *and* hakama, *a costume later adopted by scholars and the wealthy* ▶

Armour plated helmet over a cap.
The plates were usually joined with
thonging to make it ornamental.
Sixteenth century

Iron helmet. Eighteenth century

Helmet with neckguard of lined mail
with a fern leaf crest. Sixteenth
century

Samurai cap as worn under a helmet
until the end of the eighteenth
century. The long hair beneath was
tied in a bunch with the queue at the
top

Helmet with crest and side plates

Samurai woman with a coolie-type hat covered with a veil to conceal her face. The long kimono is hitched up with a sash

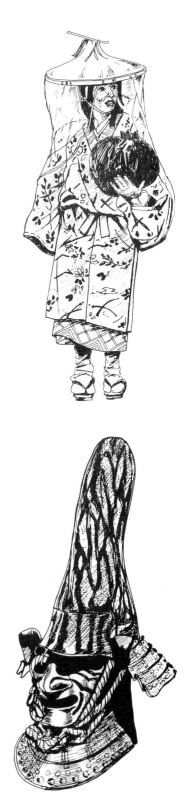

Samurai dress worn with full armour, of the late twelfth to late fourteenth centuries

A warriors' whole face mask

Woman of the samurai class, covering her face with an elaborate headdress known as ichime-gasa, resembling an umbrella. To shorten their kimono they tied them up with a sash

Helmet in the form of a court cap of the late sixteenth century

PLATE 1   *The man on the* left *is wearing a* yukata *with a simple*
obi. *(Large patterned fabrics are worn by boys, whilst small designs
are reserved for adults.) He is also wearing* tabi *and* geta.
The girl in the centre *is wearing a* tsukesage *kimono with the design
originating from the base. The* obi *and* obiage *colours harmonise with
the bamboo grove pattern.*
The woman on the right *is dressed in a* kurotomosode *with five crests.
This is one of the most common types of* kimono *for married women.
Both women are wearing* tabi *and* zori

PLATE 2   The tea ceremony. The tea caddy held in the girl's hand is about 5 cm high; the jar holds the powdered tea. A small strip of bamboo is usually used as a spoon. The portable brazier could be of clay or metal and stands on a bedding board. The tea kettle is of iron. The girls are wearing plain kimono *and have little hair ornamentation. The man in the* background *is wearing a* hakama

PLATE 3   The samurai on the left is wearing a hitatare and
hakama. He is carrying a cross-headed spear in his hand and two
swords in his belt. His sandals are made of straw. The iron helmet has
golden metal ornamentation.

The man on the right is wearing a yoroi-hitatare. The armour on his
legs and helmet lying beside him is composed of metal plates or bamboo
held together with lacing. This method offers great protection from
attacks with arrows and sword thrusts. The fan held in his hand is
carried in battle, the iron end plates used to ward off an enemy's
weapons.

The central figure is wearing a kataginu, a sleeveless upper garment,
now known as the kamishimo, it was worn over a kimono and
combined with hakama pulled up as for marching orders

PLATE 4   *The geisha in the* background *is elegantly dressed in a* kimono. *Her hair is in a chignon style with* kogai *and* kushi. *The girl on the* left *is performing a geisha dance, holding a fan. She is wearing a dark formal* kimono *with the* obi *matching the colour of the design of the kimono.*

The maiko *on the* right *is tightly bound into her* kimono *by an* obi. *She is carrying a decorated hat.*

Her hair is profusely ornamented with kushi *and pins*

PLATE 5   Nō *costumes have been so refined throughout the centuries that they have become stylised; perfect in every detail including the method of wearing. The actor on the* right *is dressed in white underclothes on top of which he wears a plain silk garment, the colour of the collar indicating the character played; and over this a gold brocade* atsuita *as well as a wig and mask.*

The figure in the background *is from kabuki. The colour and pattern of the dress denotes the character portrayed. This 'red' princess is in a red kimono with a fan-shaped tiara in her hair. The obi is in a contrasting dark colour. The make-up is heavy and is part of the costume. As in all kabuki, a wig is worn.*

The figure in the foreground *is from one of kabuki's most popular stories –* The Village School. *The costume is that of a retainer in white and turquoise mourning clothes*

PLATE 6 *The little boy on the right is in a parade dressed as a courtier, in silk robes consisting of* haori *and* hakama. *The golden headwear rests on a padded cushion and is held in place with ribbons and cord.*

The young boy on the left is dressed for a Shinto dance.

He is wearing a red wig, the colour of bravery and passion, and a red haori *over a* kimono.

The figure in the centre is performing a dance based on the legend of a Chinese warrior. The mask is intended to terrify his enemies. In the background can be seen the gohei *or carp streamers*

PLATE 7   Tattooing or irezumi *is used to give personality to the body. The design covers the entire back, upper arms and thighs, leaving the chest free, but giving the impression of a very short jacket. With the completely tattooed set of 'clothes' all that is required to be considered dressed is a loincloth. It can take more than one year to tattoo a whole body and is very costly. The designs are traditional and include dragons, folk heroes and landscapes. Nude figures are never portrayed*

PLATE 8   The bride on the left is wearing a uchikake. The design of cranes and waves is popular for festive occasions. Beneath this is worn a pastel coloured kimono. Her hair is profusely decorated with kogai and kushi. The lady on the right is wearing a hat decorated with flowers. She is also wearing an uchikake made of wadded silk. The cotton filling at the hemline weighs the garment down to give it an elegant flow. The bridegroom is dressed formally in a five-crested black haori with white cords. Beneath this he wears both a white and a black under-kimono. The hakama is of black and white striped silk. Both bride and groom are carrying folded fans. the bride's with a tassel at the end. All these figures are wearing white tabi with zori, the formal footwear, with white straps

The black lacquered cap of a dancer

The samurai was probably the finest type of hereditary soldier in the world. But in the Edo period (1603-1867) he also had a defined civil status with the power to carry two swords, one official and one personal, the official one being removed when seated.

Samurai armour was constructed of metal plates or bamboo strips held together with lacing. Whilst looking dignified it was still a good protection against swords and arrows.

The samurai in their new status as rulers developed their own mode of dress. The *eboshi* and *ori-eboshi* caps were worn in preference to the *kammuri* caps worn by the courtiers, and the *suō* robe replaced the *hō* of the courtiers. The *suō* was a costume adopted in the fifteenth century as formal attire for soldiers. It consisted of a *hitatare* jacket and *hakama* with extremely long and wide trousers. When worn by the samurai the jacket, usually made of cloth rather than silk had an heraldic crest in five specific places – behind the neck, on the middle of the sleeves, and on the front and back. For theatrical wear the term *suō* was applied to the jacket only.

After the war, in the sixteenth century, freedom of dress was also available to the men. The robes and the *kosode* had such decorative designs that they were hard to distinguish from the female garments, and far less believable that they were worn by military leaders.

The *jimbaori* vest worn on campaigns was also elaborate.

The dress of the samurai also reflected their rank. For formal occasions the attire consisted of the *kamishimo*, a combination of 'upper and lower', being very wide at the shoulders and

The suō *robe, similar to the* hitatare, *but made in a cheaper cloth, is seen here worn with an* eboshi-cap

Back view

33

pulled in at the waist. The short, sleeveless overjacket or *kataginu* for the court ranks had stiffened shoulder pieces and the *hakama* had a very low crotch and side openings. The *hakama* were held in place by two sets of ties, one in front and one at the back, fastening around the waist.

The *kami-shimo* was worn over a *kimono* and with the *hakama* completed the ceremonial attire for samurai of high rank. When the occasion was less formal, the hem of the *hakama* was raised from the ground. All ranks normally wore the *hakama* short, ending just above the ground for everyday wear, whereas for special occasions the higher ranking warriors wore the *naga-hakama* trailing to the ground. These were extremely impractical, requiring special skill for walking, and were worn mainly as a status symbol.

When on official journeys the mounted samurai wore the *hakama* and a three quarter length *haori* instead of the *kataginu*. A black varnished flat conical hat protected the wearers from the elements. Those on foot wore a type of knee breeches with leggings, and the coat, lifted at the back by the sword, gave a characteristic silhouette.

The samurai dress was sombre in colour – dull blues, greys and browns, plain or with small designs was general.

For winter wear trousers were lined. The two dates for changing into summer or winter attire were always clearly defined as the fifth day of the fifth month into summer apparel and the first day of the ninth month back into winter clothes.

When off duty the samurai generally wore *kimono* without the *haori* or *hakama*, and often hid their faces beneath a deep basket-like hat. A characteristic hairstyle of the samurai was a shaven head at the crown, the back and side hair gathered into a queue, well oiled and doubled over the crown and tied tightly. It was also important for the hair to be well trimmed, giving clean cut ends.

Low ranking samurai known as the *doshin*, maintained their own individual style of dress, wearing only one sword and no *hakama*. Even on ceremonial occasions they were only dressed in their everyday garb.

As their symbol of office, which included patrolling the streets, they carried a *jitte*, a weighted steel chain with a hook, in order to catch the sword blade or knife of an attacker. If any real trouble arose they would sit on horseback with chain body armour beneath their *kimono*, and a flat lacquered or iron-plated helmet.

Hakama, *type of loose trousers, so pleated to give the appearance of a skirt. They can be unlined or lined but never padded*

Characteristic hairstyle of a samurai with shaven crown and the side hair tightly bound in a queue and brought forward

THE AINU

An Ainu hunter

The Ainu, an aboriginal tribe who mainly inhabit the northern parts of the island of Hokkaido, are a sturdy race, flat faced with a heavy jaw line, the men with a profusion of black hair and long beards.

The women often tattooed moustaches above their upper lips, the incisions being filled with soot, which is regarded as a sacred substance, to protect them from evil spirits. They wear many earrings, bracelets and necklaces made of metal discs or ropes of beads. Both men and women wear much the same kind of dress. The *kimono*, made of elm bark fibre or of a cotton fabric, is shorter than that of the Japanese, with a narrower sash.

Except in winter, when salmon-skin foot covering is worn, they are mainly bare footed.

A garment worn by the Ainu men, known as *atushi*, is made of the thin bark of the atsui tree which is woven into a cloth. The raffia type material has coarse pieces of cotton applied with diagonal lines of cotton threads.

Their coats are of bear skin, the collar decorated with red and blue cloth with green and white trimmings. Their caps are of a coarse linen with fox fur lining.

Ceremonial dress, once made of animal skins, is now more often made of cloth of grass fibres or thin bark, patterned with geometrical shapes in bright colours.

As a sign of mourning women wear hoods and cut their hair short.

An Ainu wearing a short kimono

35

An Ainu girl with tattooed lips and a
moustache

An Ainu's fur coat made of bear skin
trimmed with cloth and cord

A well dressed Ainu in a kimono
made of elm bark fibre

A bearded Ainu chieftain wearing
an embroidered kimono

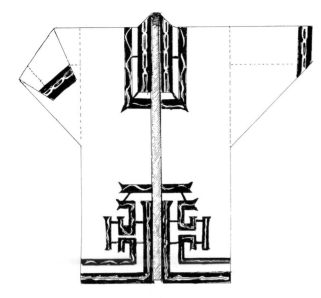

An Ainu man's garment made from
the bark of the atsuita tree with
cotton cloth ornamentation and
embroidery

Ainu woman's garment seen from the
back, made of thin strips of bark
with embroidery and appliqué. The
sleeves are tapered and a seam,
centre back, can also be seen

Ainu's cap made of a coarse cotton
with fox fur lining

GEISHA GIRLS

The Chino-Japanese word *geisha* means a person of pleasing accomplishments. Geisha girls are professional entertainers who sing and dance at restaurants and clubs or act as hostesses. They must be able to make good conversation as well as to do flower arranging and perform with expertise the traditional tea ceremony. Many also play the *samisen* which is a three-stringed guitar. An education for all this can take years, sometimes beginning as early as the age of seven. They are elegant, often wearing an embroidered cloak or *haori* over a brightly coloured *kimono* and *obi*. They use whitening to make up their already pale faces and to accentuate the lines of their eyes and mouth.

Wigs are necessary for special geisha dances and these are elaborately coiffured into a shape known as 'split peach'. To preserve this style for ten days or so without having to re-arrange it they sleep with their necks resting on specially shaped wooden blocks.

The *maiko* are pupils who wait on the geisha girls. They wear particularly elaborate hair styles and brightly coloured *kimono*.

The Kyoto New Year procession of geisha and their maiko is one of the sights of Japan.

Playing the samisen

A geisha girl's elaborate hairstyle known as 'split peach'. This is dressed every ten days or so

A geisha girl doing a Kabuki dance with a fan

Young maiko, *in her final year of training, with an elaborate hairstyle*

The wig of a maiko in her last stage of training

A maiko or pupil geisha girl wearing geta

NŌ AND KABUKI THEATRE COSTUME

The so-called dark ages of Japanese literature, from the early part of the fourteenth century to the seventeenth century produced the classic Nō drama, performed mainly for the upper classes. Its origins are ascribed to a religious dance of a pantomime character called Kagara, associated with Shintō ceremonials.

To dispel the pessimism displayed in the stately and tragic dance of the Nō, the Kyōgen (mad words) which was pure farce, was played during the interludes, and later the Kabuki which grew from the demand of the 'workers' who wanted to enjoy comedy and were excluded from the aristocratic Nō and Kyōgen.

Actors became very much leaders of fashion. The Nō theatre adopted everyday dress through the custom of patrons giving a garment to an artist, which was then elaborated. The shape of the garment became important in width and length as well as the position of the attachment of the sleeves and openings, as these dictated the arm movements used.

Actor in the role of the ghost of a general

Other important features such as the stiffness or softness of the material and the type of decoration, and whether the robe was lined or unlined, all governed the role for which a garment was worn.

Costumes of the utmost magnificence were worn. All parts were enacted by men, women having been banned from the stage by the Tokugawa shogunate in 1629. The costumes, unchanged for centuries, are handed down through the families.

In the context of Nō, the word *happi* refers to a garment usually known as *hō*, worn by persons of rank. It is an outer garment and was given to Nō players as a gift. A lined *happi* is used for demon gods or generals in battle attire, whilst the unlined version is worn by the noblemen in battle.

The *sobatsugi* is a lined and sleeveless happi which represents armour. From the late sixteenth century Nō costumes were

A Kabuki actor

A costume worn by Nō actors depicting a member of the Imperial family

made specifically for their performances and the use of heavier *karaori* was developed. *Karaori*, literally means *Chinese weave* and is a type of Nō costume still in use at the present time. The outer garment, used for female roles, is usually made of stiff, patterned, heavy brocade, originally imported from China.

Among the costumes worn for female roles are the *surihaku* and *nuikaku* worn as undergarments with the *karaori*.

The *maiginu*, meaning dance robe, developed from the *kariginu*, and was a colourful gown worn for dancing. The sleeves were extra long, made of two widths of material. It was unlined and unstarched.

The *kariginu*, originally a garment worn by courtiers, lined or unlined, is usually made of a light loosely woven cloth. When used in Nō it is worn as an outer robe and extravagantly ornamented. When lined, it is worn for high ranking roles, and the unlined version for Shintō priest parts. The *chōken* meaning long robe, was originally worn at court with the skirts extremely long. An unstarched short version developed from the *kariginu*, which became domestic wear of nobles in the eleventh century and was later adopted by the military. It was unlined and had two-piece long sleeves. The *chōken* can also be worn for female roles.

The chōken *developed from the* kariginu *was unlined, and had two-piece long sleeves, worn for Nō performances*

Male character in a Kyōgen play. His extra long trousers denote a high rank

An atsuita, *meaning 'thick board',* kimono *in a damask is adopted for commoners or low ranking samurai in Nō plays*

A banded atsuita kimono *with coloured triangles and windmills, clouds and floral squares, worn for Nō performances in the middle of the seventeeth century*

A mask for Kyōgen made of wood, depicting a clown or jester

Robe worn by Nō and Kyōgen actors. The formal robes depict an ancient religious ceremony

Kataginu *shoulder piece for Kyōgen performance, made of hemp with a moon and Chinese bellflower design. Originally a servants' sleeveless jacket, it was adopted in the late sixteenth century as semi-formal court dress*

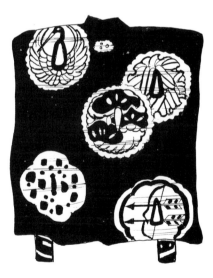

A silk kataginu *worn in a Kyōgen play. The stencil dyed design depicts sword guards*

The *kataginu*, worn for Kyōgen, was without sleeves, made of hemp. It was originally a servant's sleeveless jacket made in a coarse cloth and was adopted as a semi-formal court dress for military officers. It is usually in a bold embroidered design worn over a *kosode*.

An *atsuita*, meaning thick board, was usually plain except for a striped band at the waist. This was a gentleman's formal attire, the weft of raw silk, the warp of treated silk. In Nō it is worn by generals and demons. A similar garment, the *noshime*, of which the warp was of raw silk and the weft of treated silk, was worn beneath the *asagamishimo*, a strong outer robe made of hemp. In Nō plays the *noshime* is worn more by the ordinary people and the samurai of lower degree.

Plain *noshime* are also worn for priests and older men parts, whilst the banded versions are reserved for the samurai and lower classes.

The unlined *suō* is similar to the *hitatare* and represents everyday wear. The *hangiri*, a form of *hakama*, is worn with a *happi*.

Nō costumes have been refined in every detail from colour, pattern and cut, even the stylised method of weaving them.

In most Nō dramas there are just two main characters, a few minor ones, and a chanting chorus. The main actor or *shite* always wears white under-robes and *tabi* socks. A collar of a specific colour indicating the rank of the character is worn beneath the outer robes with a sash around the waist. An overjacket or *hakama*, a wig and headdress complete the outfit.

The bands securing the wigs are known as *katsura*, and are worn across the forehead tying in a knot at the back of the head, leaving the long ends to fall loose down the back.

Masks are the main feature of Nō drama and they are treated with awe and respect by the actors who wear them. Although masks of spirits and demons are usually very intense, the Nō masks for female parts are without expression, an inclination of the head catching the light producing a subtle change of mood.

The costumes of Kyōgen are simpler than those of Nō and so show better what the ordinary people wore in mediaeval times.

Nō costumes and the *kosode kimono* are both developments in the tradition of Japanese costume. Whilst Nō costumes are highly stylised clothes worn by nobility in the mediaeval period, Kyōgen, although stylised, depict dress worn by the ordinary person of that time.

Masks worn in Kyōgen fall into three categories: (1) for gods and demons, (2) for animals, plants and their spirits and (3) for human beings (a) Monkey (b) Angry woman (c) An actor wearing the mask of the God of Happiness (d) Old woman, also used for nun parts (e) Old man, also used for shite characters (f) Demon (g) Priest (h) Fox

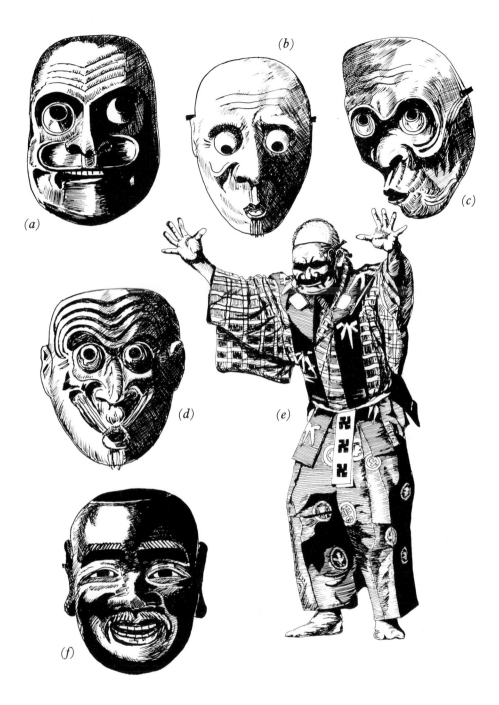

(a) Animal mask used for diverse animals such as cows, horses, dogs and crabs (b, c and d) Whistler masks. These are used in dances and mimes throughout Japan and can be worn for a variety of characters such as the spirits of birds, insects, animals and even fungi (e) A Kyōgen actor portraying a part in 'Shedding the Demon Shell' (f) God of Wealth mask

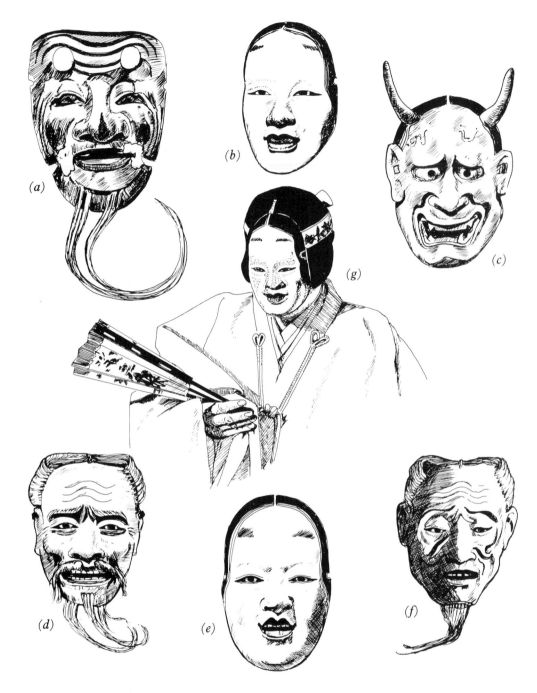

Nō masks made from Japanese cyprus are about 12mm thick and finished with thirteen layers of paint. The expresssions of the masks are both symbolic and ambiguous, and the performers' art turns the suspended expression into a definite character. (a) Old man mask (b) Middle aged or mature woman. The hair and painted eyebrows are black, the eyebrows having been shaven off and replaced higher on the forehead (c) Female demon's mask, the horns denote anger (d) Woodcutter or fisherman (e) Young girl's mask (f) Happy old man (g) Female mask and wig secured with a special band

(a) Mask used in the role of a dragon god (b) Young lay priest mask (c) Violent demon mask, a devil in human form (d) A god in human disguise with a moustache (e) Aged god or sorrowful ghost (f) Old man mask

(a)

(b)

(c)

(d)

(e)

(f)

Mask and wig worn in a Nō play. the wig is secured by a band placed across the forehead and tied in a knot behind, the long ends falling down the back

Nuihaku for a Nō performance. The plum blossom trellis design upper and lower part is separated by a gold leaf pattern of interlocking lozenges enclosing flower heads

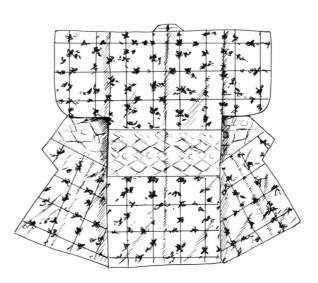

A lined kariginu *of the middle of the seventeeth century worn for Nō. It is worn over another robe*

A furisode in a tie-dye design. Most of the inner edge of the sleeves are unattached, and this style is worn in certain Nō dances

Kataginu *shoulder piece of the late ▶ seventeenth century, dyed with a gourd and bamboo fence design, used in Kyōgen*

◀ *Female character in a Kyōgen play. The conventional costume is a brightly coloured* kimono *tied at the waist with a narrow sash and a long narrow strip of white cloth wrapped around the head, the ends hanging down either side below the waist*

Kyōgen costume is indicative of the type of character, as opposed to expressing the individual person. For example a *daimyō* would wear a tall black hat, a broadly striped *kimono* under a cloak with broad sleeves and long trousers.

A woman would be seen in a brightly patterned *kimono* with a narrow sash and a white cloth around her head, the ends hanging either side. The individual characters are created mainly by movements and intonation of voice.

Kyōgen does not make use of masks to the extent of the Nō plays. In Kyōgen they are used mainly for gods and demons, and animals, plants and spirits. One of the most used and versatile properties used is a fan, folded or open.

The Kabuki costumes are one of its most charming aspects of the performance. Special patterns and colours are designated for each role, so that the character is easily recognisable. The townspeople normally are dressed in a plain *kimono* with their *mon* or family crests on the centre back, on the sleeves and on either side of the chest.

The upper classes are depicted wearing more luxurious costumes, larger wigs and more hair ornamentation. The colours also indicate the good from the bad characters portrayed.

The Gagaku-Bugata court entertainment which came to Japan in the seventh century from China, also had very elaborate costumes, the musicians wearing white robes and black helmets of the Chinese T'ang dynasty, whilst the dancers were dressed in brocade and full, richly embroidered trousers, looking similar to skirts.

Actor dressed as a daimyō *in a Kyōgen performace*

A Kabuki actor completing his make-up and setting his wig into place

Of the late seventeenth century this kataginu *is made of hemp with a design of gourds and half-wheels*

CHILDREN

Child dressed for the New Year Fire Festival ready to pull the fairy-tale floats

Scarlet and orange were the main colours of the large patterned fabrics in which babies were dressed. Little girls especially looked like large butterflies or birds of paradise.

At about four weeks old babies were taken to visit a temple, and were dressed in long elaborate ceremonial clothes on which the family crest was embroidered. They were given an amulet or wooden charm by the priest, which was then worn in an embroidered or brocade bag tied around the child's waist.

There are many special days for Japanese children. On 15 November *Shichigosan* is celebrated. The word means seven, five, three. Girls dressed in brightly coloured *kimono* are presented at the shrines of Shintō diety at the age of three and seven, and boys at the age of five when they are considered to enter various periods of their lives.

The first is 'band removing'. This consists of removing the narrow ribbon-like band sewn to their clothes which tie them to their body, and replacing them with an *obi*, similar to that worn by adults.

The second phase, for boys only, is the wearing of the *hakama*, and the third phase is allowing their hair to grow long, which in infancy is always shaved off in the belief of strengthening the hair. At each of these three stages the children are taken to their guardian god or patron shrine.

It was from the late seventeenth to the early eighteenth centuries, that children were allowed for the first time to grow their hair long. Boys at the age of five ceremoniously wore their first *hakama*, whilst girls from the age of seven were first permitted to wear a formal *obi*, rather than a simple one of cord.

The *Hina-matsuri*, Festival of Little People (or Dolls) is on 3 March when small girls are dressed in ceremonial attire to celebrate this day with a large display of dolls in their houses, often heirlooms depicting the Imperial Court.

The *Koi* (Carp) Festival on 5 May is for the little boys who surround themselves with toys. All boys take part in this

Child dressed for the festival at the Sumiyoshi shrine

festival which is marked by symbols of manhood drawn from the martial past including banners, swords and miniature sets of armour. This is now known as Children's Day, and large paper streamers hollowed out in the shape of a carp, symbolising strength and determination, are suspended from poles.

One of the most colourful of recent festivals, celebrated 15 January is Adult's Day or Coming of Age Day, known as *Seijin-no-hi*, when young men and women have reached the age of twenty, dress in their best clothes, the traditional *kimono*, and are welcomed into adult life. They visit their shrines and light candles.

Headwear of a child dressed for the New Baby Heron Dance held every July at the Yasaka Shrine in Kyoto, inspired by the four hundred year old Dance of the Adult Herons

Young boy at a modern 'cram' school wearing a headband reading 'struggle to pass'

Girl playing the koto, *a native instrument*

Young girl gathering the tea leaves after the June rains

A young baby strapped on the back of his young sister who is wearing geta

Small girl street singer with her ▶ *gekkin slung behind her, wearing a coolie type hat and geta*

◀ *Little girl strolling player, playing a guitar-like gekkin*

TATTOOING

Back view of a fully tattooed body wearing a belt and loin cloth

Tattooing or *irezumi* has a long and chequered history in Japan. The early primitive designs indicated difference of rank, later becoming just ornamental. It was most popular in the seventeenth and eighteenth centuries. During this period merchants who were not allowed to wear fine silks, brocode or precious ornaments, did however tattoo themselves secretly. Later tattooing was confined to the lower classes, often used as imitation clothing by the poor; even becoming an instrument of punishment.

As some stenuous work necessitated a bare body, tattooing was adopted instead of clothing. This was so designed to camouflage and adorn the nakedness so all that was required was a loin cloth.

The designs were traditional, including the dragon, landscapes and flowers, also human and animal figures as well as birds. In the nineteenth and twentieth centuries tattooing was associated with particular groups such as fishmongers, gamblers and gangsters.

Tattooing still flourishes in certain areas of Japan. A complete design covers the back, buttocks, upper arm and thighs, leaving the stomach area clear. The main tint is black which turns blue under Japanese skins.

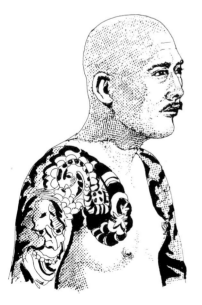

Tattooing on shoulder and upper arm showing Japanese mythology

HEADWEAR AND HAIRSTYLES

The shimada *formal coiffure. the hair is gathered and tied near the crown with some added false hair, and the tip folded forward. The chignon is formed by spreading out the hair*

Throughout the Middle Ages it was the custom for men to wear beards and long moustaches which they tended most carefully, but this custom was reversed in the sixteenth century and even today Japanese men do not allow hair to grow on their faces. Both sexes shave off any trace of down even from their lips, cheeks and forehead, as well as from their earlobes and noses.

Japanese women's most important ornament was their own black hair which was carefully arranged with pins, mainly with two prongs, made of ivory, horn, wood or metal and kept glossy and supple with pomade or oil. It was richly decorated with curved-back tortoiseshell combs or bars as well as fresh flowers.

The 'inverted maidenhair' style is one of the most popular and informal ones for women. The hair is tied at the roots, divided into two tresses that are looped and brought back behind the crown. The sides and back hair is then puffed and held in place with hairpins around a chignon.

The formal coiffure, the *shimada* or rounded chignon, has the hair tied at the crown with the loop wrapped around an ornamental cloth with a small bar through the two sides of the loop. The hair is then spread into a chignon. A small wad of cotton encased in a paper pillow is placed under the chignon to hold it in place. The bar protrudes about 1 cm either side of the chignon. Gold and silver as well as tortoiseshell was used for hair ornamentation by the end of the seventeenth century, although in fact prohibited at that time by various sumptuary laws.

The size and quality of decoration became greater, the most important being the *kushi* which is an elaborate comb with pendant decorations.

Except for the hair ornaments and obi fasteners, Japanese women wear no jewellery.

Until the middle of the nineteenth century men had small queues on top of their heads. They shaved the crown and tied the remaining hair at the top with paper strips, bringing the

Very young girl wearing an elaborately decorated hairstyle, holding a bamboo and paper umbrella

Ornamental bars, combs and bands,
made of ivory, tortoiseshell, wood,
silver and lacquer

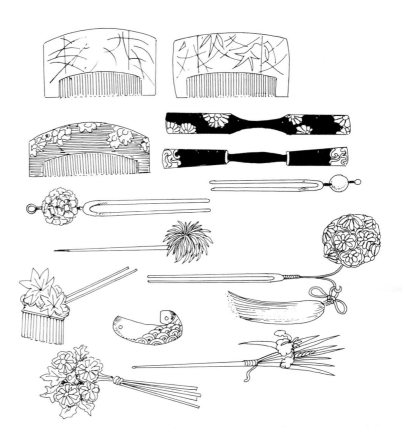

The 'inverted maidenhair' style: the
hair is divided into two tresses that
are looped, turned down and brought
behind the crown and then tied
together. This informal coiffure does
not require any false hair to be added

The 'rounded chignon' is formed by
tying the hair at the crown and
making a loop at the end and then
wrapped with an ornamental cloth.
A small paper pillow is placed
beneath the chignon to hold it in
place, part of the loop appearing
each side of the chignon to display the
ornamental material

Shrine maiden in a hairstyle
decorated for the sacred kagura dance

55

queue forward over the forehead and fastening it with the same strip so that the queue was tied tightly to the first knot. There were several fashions for making these queues, which had to be untied and remade every few days.

After 1868 the queues were cropped, and at first the hair was left fairly long, hiding half the ears, but gradually it was cut shorter.

Painting the face was customary for men and women throughout Japan. The women painted their faces with a thick paste of white powder. A pale complexion in women was a sign of beauty. The white stain was acquired artificially by using *nukabukuro*, which are small cotton bags containing rice powder. This was moistened with perfumed water before smoothing it over the face, neck and upper part of the breasts during the day, and over the whole body after a bath.

Large straw hat worn over a kerchief as protection against the sun

It was also fashionable for women to make the mouth look smaller by putting a red spot in the centre of the lower lip by means of a paste obtained by crushing the flower petals of *carthamus tinctuna*, a kind of saffron.

When young girls reached womanhood, their eyebrows were shaved or plucked and black marks were painted with soot high on the forehead. In ancient times men of rank blackened their teeth as a sign of high birth. They regarded black, being the only colour that never changes, as a token of constancy and fidelity.

Women seldom wore any headwear in order not to disarrange their elaborate coiffures. The large chignon acted as protection against the climatic conditions. However, in winter a long shawl would sometimes act as a hood. In summer they would carry large golden coloured straw hats that could be worn over kerchiefs as a protection against the sun. Sunshades were made of bamboo frames covered with silk, linen or glazed paper.

Street vendors wore flattish round hats made of bamboo sheaths, whilst coolies wore and sometimes still do wear mushroom-shaped hats made of spliced bamboo covered with a cloth.

Young girl with her face and neck painted with a white powder and a red spot on the lower lip to make the mouth look smaller

FOOTWEAR

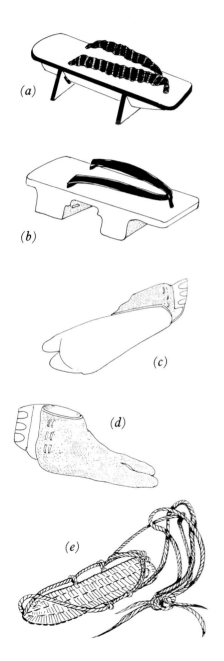

(a)

(b)

(c)

(d)

(e)

Footwear for men and women consists of *tabi* which are white cotton socks with padded soles and a separate division for the big toe in order to hold in place the thongs of the wooden shoes or hemp sandals.

Geta are unique to Japan. They have raised wooden soles and, like the hemp sandals, are held in place with thonging. The *zori*, another style of sandal, has flat straw soles which are worn as fomal footwear with ceremonial *kimono*.

In summer linen stockings are worn and in the winter these are made of wool. Flat plaited straw sandals, *waraji*, are worn in dry weather, but in bad, wooden pattens or *geta* are more usual.

Clogs are made either of plain wood or matting. Plain clogs consist of a piece of oblong wood, the ends sometimes rounded, supported by two flat oblong wooden parts running across, one behind the other. The hole in the front has a loop of thonging through which is passed a longer piece with the ends at the holes either side towards the rear of the sole. The top thong is held between the big toe and second toe.

Clogs vary in height. The sole and supports may be carved in one piece. Mat clogs are similarly made, the matting being of woven rushes.

Farmers wear *jikatabi*, cloven stocking-like footwear with rubber soles. These cling tightly to the foot and it is still customary for farmers and other such workers to wear these today.

(a and b) Plain geta *(c and d)* Tabi *made with a thick cotton sole covered in calico reaching the ankle. They are held on by small metal clasps catching a cord behind the heel (e) Straw sandal or* zori *used for long walks. The straw thong is tied over the toes and around the ankle*

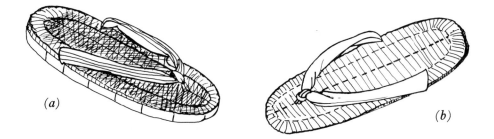

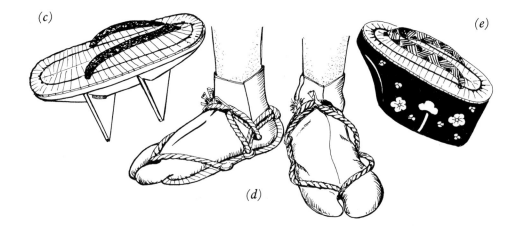

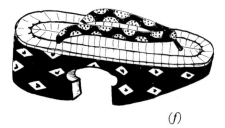

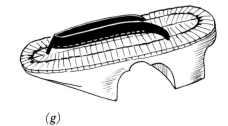

*(a and b) Sandal of matting or straw
lined on the sole with strands of hemp
(c) Geta made of matted rushes (d)
Straw sandals worn over tabi
(e and f) Decorated geta made of
matting with cotton covering (g)
Geta with matted sole and wooden
support*

GLOSSARY OF COSTUME TERMS

Young girl in a formal layered
furisode

Asagamishimo	Unlined outer robe made of hemp
Atsuita	Stiff gold and brocaded silk outer robe for men's roles in Nō
Atushi	Garment made of thin bark of the atsui tree
Awase	Lined robe without wadding
Chōken	Semi formal dress of high ranking samurai or generals. Outer robe of silk gauze worn by male and female dance roles in Nō
Daimon	Shogun or *daimyō's* formal costume consisting of wide sleeved jacket with family crests
Daimyō	Rich merchant, feudal lord through whom the samurai controlled most areas of Japan between the fourteenth and fifteenth centuries
Dangawari	Parts of varying textiles sewn together to form a garment
Eboshi	Nobleman, samurai or court official's lacquered hat
Eboshi-cap	Ceremonial cap worn by warriors from the fourteenth to sixteenth centuries
Edo okumi	Edo decoration along the edges of a garment
Fukuro obi	Pouched or double folded *obi*
Furisode	Literally means 'swinging sleeves'. A deep sleeve not attached to the garment along the lower inner edge, a long sleeved type of *kimono*
Gohei	Pendant paper cutting
Geta	Formal wooden footwear designed to keep the feet clean. The flat wooden sole is raised by two strips of wood, and kept on with two pieces of thonging passing between the first and second toes, dividing over the top of the foot

Hakama	Pleated and divided skirt made in fine stripes worn by men on ceremonial occasions, and by the courtiers and samurai. A wide trouser-like attire, similar to culottes
Hangiri	*Hakama* with wide leg openings and stiffened back, made of a single coloured cloth patterned in gold
Haori	Short overcoat fastened in front with ties
Happi	Cotton coat, usually thigh length. In Nō context it is usually an outer robe, symbolising armour
Hirosode	Literally means 'big or wide sleeves'. A type of *kimono*
Hitatare	Samurai's large square-cut coat with cord laced sleeve edges. Ceremonial robe for court nobles
Hitoe-happi	Unlined happi
Hō	An outer robe
Inrō	Miniature medicine box or set of inter-locking compartments hung from an *obi* by a silk cord
Irezumi	The art of tattooing
Jak tabi	Similar to a *geta*
Jikatabi	Cloven stocking-like footwear with rubber soles
Jimbaori	Sleeveless battle coat or campaign jacket worn over armour
Juni-hitoe	Literally means 'twelve unlined robes'. These were worn one over the other. Court lady's costume for formal occasions from the late eighth to the end of the twelfth centuries
Kabuki	Popular Japanese drama incorporating music and dance. The first performance was in a Kyoto theatre in 1603
Kake shitaobi	An outer *obi*
Kamishimo	Samurai costume consisting of ankle length *hakama* and *katiginu* worn over a *kimono*
Kammuri	Hat worn by nobles and court officers in classical plays, crown or coronet
Karaori	Literally means 'Chinese weave'. Silk brocaded outer robe for upper class women's parts in Nō

Inrō *with a design of horses at pasture and monkeys. Late seventeeth century*

Jimbaori *of the late sixteenth century. The campaign jacket could be worn over armour*

60

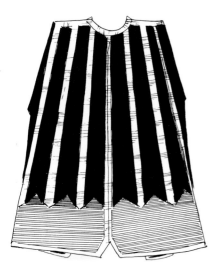

A jimbaori *of the late sixteenth century*

Kariginu	Loose short jacket with abbreviated sleeves worn as outermost garment of *juni-hitoe*. A hunting outfit in vogue from the eighth to the twelfth centuries
Kasane-gi	Set of clothing
Kataginu	Short sleeveless garment made of hemp with bold patterns and broad wing-like shoulder pieces
Katamigawari	Sections of different materials or textiles sewn together at random to make the pattern of the garment
Katsugi	Outer robe that can also act as hood and cover the head
Kimono	Long loose robe or wrap
Kogai	Type of hairpin, a bar shaped ornament
Koshimaki	Literally means 'waist wrapper'. Formally a loincloth or petticoat, but became a long robe in the seventeenth century
Kosode	Means 'small sleeves' or 'short sleeves'. The standard size *kimono* of today, formerly an undergarment. Could be of padded silk
Kurotomosode	Black, short sleeved *kimono*
Kushi	Comb
Kyōgen	Fictitious and comedy plays
Maiginu	Silk gauze robe for female roles in Nō drama
Mino	Coat made of straw
Mompe	Loose trousers worn for work by women
Mon	Family crest
Nae-eboshi	Young person's headwear
Nō	The word means 'accomplishment' or 'performance'. Classical drama formed in the fourteenth century. Kanami, the creator, died in 1384. The actors wear masks and are very stylised in manner and dress, accompanied by chorus and flute and drum music
Noshime	Robes worn in Nō drama, in striped or check materials, and generally with a pattern across the midriff
Nuihaku	Women's robes in no drama, also a material to which to glue gold or silver foil with a stencil and also embroidery

Lined kariginu *with a design of leaf roundels worn for Nō performances*

Obi	Deep sash
Obi-age	Piece of fine silk used to conceal the small cushion padding out the bow at the back of the *obi*. Band for holding *obi* in place
Ori-eboshi cap	Folded eboshi of lacquered paper
Osode	Literally means 'wide sleeves'. A type of *kimono*
Samurai	Warriors who were originally members or retainers of dominant families whose power increased with the decline of the central government between the ninth and eleventh centuries
Sashiko	Quilted jacket or coat
Shimada	Woman's bouffant hairstyle
Shite	Principal Nō actor
Shogun	Title granted in 1192 meaning 'barbarian conquering great general'
Shogunate	Government of a shogun
Suō	Formal middle rank dress, usually including jacket and *hakama*. Wide sleeved top garment, warrior's robe from the fourteenth to the late sixteenth centuries
Surihaku	Gold or silver leaf imprint on silk; a *kimono* thus decorated
Tabi	Socks with split toes
Uchikake	Long outer robe worn by females dating from the mid fourteenth century
Waraji	Plaited straw sandals
Water-ire	Wadded *kimono*
Yoroi-hitatare	Warrior costume consisting of hitatare and short pleated hakama worn under armour
Yukata	Unlined light informal summer *kimono*, usually made of boldly patterned cotton, dark blue and white being the most popular colours
Zori	Formal shoes, the flat soles made of woven straw, rush, flax and bamboo, and covered in either fabric or leather, held on with thonging, passing between the first and second toes, dividing over the top of the foot

The uchikake, *a full length formal and elegant outer robe worn by noblewomen until the beginning of the seventeeth century, is now part of traditional bridal dress. The* uchikake *is made of wadded silk with long sleeves, the cotton filling gives substance to the hemline. This is worn over a* kakeshita kimono *and* obi

BIBLIOGRAPHY

BRADSHAW, ANGELA, *World Costume*, Black 1952

BRAIN, ROBERT, *The Decorated Body*, Harper and Row 1979

BRUHN, W, and TILKE, M, *Pictorial History of Costume*, Zwemmer 1955

DUNN, C J, *Everyday Life in Traditional Japan*, Batsford 1969

GILBERT, JOHN, *National Costumes of the World*, Hamlyn 1972

HAMMERTON, J A, *Lands and Peoples*, Amalgamated Press 1927

HAMMERTON, J A, *People of all Nations*, Amalgamated Press 1922-1924

HARROLD R and LEGG, P, *Folk Costumes of the World*, Blandford 1978

HATA, HISHASHI, *Kyōgen*, Hoikusha Publishing Company 1982

HUTCHINSON WALTER, editor, *Customs of the World*, Hutchinson 1913

INOVYE, JUKICHI, *Home Life in Tokyo*, K P I 1985

LOWE, G M, translator, *Daily Life in Japan*, Allen and Unwin 1979

MACINTYRE, MICHAEL, *The Shogun Inheritance*, Collins 1981

MARUOKA, D and YOSHIKOSHI, T, *Noh*, Hoikusha Publishing Company 1980

NOMA, SEIROKU, *Japanese Costumes and Textiles*, Weatherhill/Heibonsha 1974

REYNOLDS, J H and COXHEAD, G E S, editors *The Story of the World*, Universal Textbooks 1944

SHAVER, RUTH M, *Kabuki Costume*, Tuttle 1966

TILKE, M, *Costume Patterns and Designs*, Zwemmer 1956

TILKE, M, *Folk Costumes*, Zwemmer 1978

TOITA, YASUJI AND CHAKI YOSHIDA, *Kabuki*, Hoikusha Publishing Company 1981

TSUTOMU, EMA, *A Historical Sketch of Japanese Customs and Costumes*, Kokusai Bunka Shinkokai, Tokyo 1938

WATSON, W, editor, *The Great Japan Exhibition*, Royal Academy of Arts, Weidenfeld and Nicolson 1981

YAMANAKA, NORIO, *The Book of the Kimono*, Kodansha International 1982

INDEX

Numerals in *italics* refer to illustrations

Asagamishimo 43
Ashinaka 11
Atsuita *42*, 43, colour plate 5

Bow, arrow *23*; butterfly 21; chidori 22; drum 22; plover 22; plump sparrow 22; standing arrow 22; tateya 22

Chignon 54, *54*, *55*, 56, colour plate 4
Choken 41, *41*
Clogs 11, 14, 57
Crest 11, *13*, 21, 24, *25*, *26*, *29*, 33, 49, 50, colour plate 8

Daimon *29*
Daimyō 28, *49*, 49
Dangawari 18
Doshin 34

Eboshi *29*, 33, *33*

Fan 21, *29*, 49, colour plates 1, 3, 4 and 8
Fukuro obi *18*, *22*, *26*
Furisode 17, 18, *19*, 21, *23*, *48*, *59*

Geisha 38, *38*, *39*, colour plate 4
Gekkin *3*, *9*, *52*
Geta 11, *39*, 57, *57*, 59

Hairstyle 7, 21, 34, 35, 38, 49, 50, 54, 55, 56
Hakama *13*, *15*, 16, 21, 24, *26*, 27, 28, *30*, 33, *34*, 34, 43, 50, colour plates 2, 3, 6 and 8
Hangiri 43
Haori *12*, *13*, 21, *26*, *27*, 34, 38, colour plate 6
Happi 11, *11*, *13*, *14*, 40, 43
Hat 7, 11, 21, 27, *32*, 34, 49, 56, colour plate 8
Headwear *5*, *10*, 28, *32*, colour plate 6
Hirosode 17, 18
Hitatare 28, *28*, 33, 43, colour plate 3
Hō 33, 40

Inrō *60*
Irezumi 53, colour plate 7
Iro tomosode 24

Jacket 11, 14, 21, 33, 57
Jikatabi 57
Jimbaori 33, *60*, *61*
Jitte 34
Juni hitoe 27, *27*, 28

Kabuki 10, 22, *39*, 40, 49, colour plate 5
Kamishimo 33, 34, colour plate 3
Kammuri 27, 33
Karaori 41
Kariginu 16, *16*, 41, *41*, *48*, 61
Kasane-gi 15
Kataginu 34, 43, colour plate 3
Katasuso 16, 20
Katsugi 15
Katsura 43
Kimono 4, *4*, 7, *7*, *8*, 10, 11, *13*, 14, 15, 16, 17, *17*, 18, *18*, *19*, 20, 21, *21*, 22, 23, *23*, 24, 27, 28, *30*, *32*, 34, 35, *35*, *36*, 28, *48*, 49, 50, 51, 57, colour plates 1, 2, 4, 5, 6 and 8
Koshimaki 15
Kosode 15, 16, *16*, 17, *17*, 18, 20, 27, 28, 33, 43
Kurotomosode 24, colour plate 1
Kushi 54, colour plates 4 and 8
Kyogen 40, *41*, *42*, 43, *43*, *44*, *48*, 49, *49*

Maiginu 41
Maiko 38, *39*, colour plate 4
Mask *32*, *42*, 43, *44*, *45*, *46*, *47*, 49, colour plates 5 and 6
Mino 15
Mo 11
Mon 49, colour plate 8

Nae eboshi 11
Naga hakama 34
Nō 10, 40, 41, *41*, *42*, 43, *46*, *47*, *48*, 49, colour plate 5
Noshime 43

Nuihaku 20, 41, *47*

Obi 15, 16, 17, *17*, 19, 20, *20*, 21, 22, 23, *23*, 24, 38, 50, colour plates 1 and 5
Obiage *19*, 21, 24, *26*, colour plate 1
Obijime *20*, 23, 24, *26*
Ori eboshi 33
Osode 17, *25*

Queue 34, 54, 55, 56

Samisen 6, 38, *38*
Sandals 11, 14, 57
Samurai *13*, 14, 24, *28*, 28, *30*, *31*, 32, 33, 34, *42*, colour plate 3
Sash 14, 15, 17, 22, 24, 28, *32*, 35, 49
Sashiko *12*
Shite 43
Shogun 7
Shogunate 28, 40
Skirt 11, 14, 18, 21, 27
Sobatsugi 40
Suikan *16*
Suō *29*, 33, *33*, 43
Surihaku 41

Tabi *26*, 43, 57, *57*, 59, colour plates 1 and 8
Tattoo 35, *36*, 51, *53*, colour plate 7
Tie dye 15
Tomosode *25*, *26*
Trousers 11, 14, 24, 33, 34, 39
Tsukesage kimono *19*, *20*, colour plate 1

Uchikake 24, *25*, *26*, 62

Veil 28, *32*

Waraji 57
Water ire 21, 24
Wig 38, *47*, 49, colour plate 5

Yoroi hitatare 28, *29*, colour plate 3
Yukata *19*, 21, colour plate 1
Yumaki 14

Zori *26*, 57, *57*, colour plate 8